Ken Griffey, Jr.

Super Center Fielder

by

Thomas S. Owens

The Rosen Publishing Group's
PowerKids Press ™
New York

Published in 1997 by The Rosen Publishing Group, Inc.
29 East 21st Street, New York, NY 10010

First Edition

Book Design: Kim Sonsky

Photo Credits: Cover and pp. 4, 7, 10, 11, 12, 15, 16, 19 © AP/Wide World Photos; p.8 © Jeff Greenberg/International Stock; p.9 © Ronn Marratea/International Stock; p. 20 © Reuters/Jeff Christensen/Archive Photos.

Owens, Tom, 1960–
     Ken Griffey, Jr. : super center fielder / Thomas S. Owens.
          p.   cm. — (Sports greats)
     Includes index.
     Summary: A brief biography of the center fielder for the Seattle Mariners, who entered professional baseball when he was only seventeen years old.
     ISBN 0-8239-5088-3
     1. Griffey, Ken, Jr.—Juvenile literature. 2. Baseball players—United States—Biography—Juvenile literature.
[1. Griffey, Ken, Jr. 2. Baseball players. 3. Afro-Americans—Biography.] I. Title. II. Series: Sports greats (New York, NY)
GV865.G69084 1997
796.357'092
[B]—dc21   9639986
                                                                                                  CIP
                                                                                                   AC

Manufactured in the United States of America

Contents

A Star Is Born

Ken Griffey, Jr., is known as one of the best players in baseball. He comes from a family of great athletes, starting with his grandfather, Joseph "Buddy" Griffey. Buddy was the first African American to play on the high school basketball team in Donora, Pennsylvania in the 1930s.

Many years later, Buddy had a son, George Kenneth "Ken" Griffey. When Ken grew up, he played **major league** (MAY-jer LEEG) baseball. He played for nineteen years, and had over 2,000 hits.

Ken had a son, George Kenneth Griffey, Jr., also known as "Junior." Junior became one of the best center fielders in major league baseball.

◀ Ken Griffey, Jr., is one of the top players in baseball.

Learning from the Best

Junior was born on November 21, 1969. His father, Ken, played for the Cincinnati Reds. Ken was away from home a lot because the Reds played teams in other cities. But when the games were at home, Junior spent a lot of time at the ballpark. He loved to watch his father play ball. He became friends with the kids of the other players. The kids played together, but they also watched their dads **practice** (PRAK-tiss). Junior learned to play baseball by watching some of the best players of the game.

Junior wanted to follow his father to the major ▶ leagues. And just a few years later, he did.

A Big Bat in Little League

Junior signed up for Little League baseball. He was so good that some coaches thought he was older than he really was.

When he was in high school, Junior played football as well as baseball. But in his senior year, he decided to play only baseball. He was usually an outfielder. He was so good that he was named an All-American. That meant that he was one of the best high-school baseball players in the United States.

Many kids who play Little League baseball ◀ have dreams of becoming major league players.

Paid to Play

Junior knew that he wanted to play **professional** (pro-FESH-un-ul) baseball like his dad. He didn't have to wait long for his dream to come true. Many **scouts** (SKOWTS) saw Junior play in high school. But the scout for the Seattle Mariners wanted Junior to play for his team. Junior became the Mariners' first draft pick, or their first choice of **amateur** (AM-uh-chur) players. He was signed, or hired, in June 1987. Less than one month after finishing high school, Junior started playing professional baseball. He was only seventeen years old.

Junior was so good that a professional baseball team signed him right after high school. His dream was coming true. ▶

Making the Majors

Junior started his professional career by playing for the Mariners' **minor league** (MY-ner LEEG) team, in Bellingham, Washington. There he learned new skills and became an even better ball player. But more than anything, Junior wanted to play in the major leagues.

Each year, the players from the minor and major leagues take part in spring training. This is when coaches decide if players will stay in the minor leagues or move up to the majors. Junior played well during the 1989 spring training. He had only played in the minor leagues for two years. His father had played for four years.

The Mariners' manager called Junior into his office and said, "You're my starting center fielder." Junior was so excited. He was in the majors, and he was going to play his favorite position!

The Mariners saw that Junior played very well. They hoped that he could help them become a winning team.

13

Griffey and Griffey

On August 29, 1990, the Mariners made history by adding Junior's father, Ken Griffey, Sr., to their team. It was the first time that a father and son had ever played on the same team at the same time.

On September 14, 1990, the Griffeys set another record. Ken hit a 402-foot home run in the first inning of the game. The next batter up was Junior. Four pitches later, Junior hit a home run too. Later, Ken teased Junior for only hitting the ball 388 feet!

Father and son played together for the Mariners for two years. ▶

All-Star Player

Every year, the major leagues hold an All-Star game. The teams that play in the All-Star games are made up of the best professional ball players. Fans vote for the players they want to see play the game. Junior has been chosen to play in the All-Star game every year since 1990. He won the All-Star's Most Valuable Player (MVP) Award in 1992. In 1994, more than 6 million fans voted for Junior to start the All-Star game. This was the largest number of votes any player had ever received at the time.

As the interest in Junior grew, so did the interest in his team, the Mariners. Soon baseball fans all over the country wanted to know more about the Mariners.

◀ Junior played so well that he had fans all over the country. These fans soon became interested in Junior's team, the Mariners, as well.

Success at Last

The Mariners were not a winning team. In fact, they had never had a winning season. But finally, in 1991, Junior helped the team get a record of 83 wins to 79 losses. For the first time ever, the Mariners had more wins than losses.

By 1995, the Mariners won first place in their **division** (dih-VIH-zhun). That meant that they had a shot at a place in the World Series—the games that decide the champions of a baseball season. They had to beat two teams to get there.

Junior set a record by hitting six home runs in the play-offs. But the Mariners missed playing in the World Series by losing four out of six games to the Cleveland Indians.

Junior helped the Mariners ▶
become a winning team.

18

Popular Player

Thousands of baseball fans like Ken Griffey, Jr. Because so many people like him, a lot of businesses hire Junior to help them sell their **products** (PRAH-dukts). Wheaties put Junior's picture on their cereal boxes. And he was in several **commercials** (kuh-MER-shulz) for the sports-shoe company Nike.

In 1989, Junior's first year in the majors, a Ken Griffey, Jr., chocolate bar was made. More than 1 million of them were sold. But Junior never even tried one. He's **allergic** (uh-LER-jik) to chocolate!

◀ Junior has been a popular ball player since he started in the major leagues.

Off the Field

Junior's wife, Melissa, grew up right near the Mariners' ballpark. But when she met Ken Griffey, Jr., she didn't know who he was. Junior was happy to meet someone who didn't know or care that he was a famous baseball player.

Junior and Melissa have a daughter, Taryn Kennedy, and a son, Trey Kenneth. Junior likes his job as a dad. He also likes to help other kids. One way he does this is by helping the Make-a-Wish Foundation, which grants wishes to kids who are very sick.

Junior loves playing professional baseball. He also loves being able to help other people.

Glossary

allergic (uh-LER-jik) When someone has a certain reaction to a usually harmless thing.

amateur (AM-uh-chur) A person who does something for fun, not for money.

commercial (kuh-MER-shul) A message selling something on television or the radio that is played between programs.

division (dih-VIH-zhun) A grouping of teams.

major league (MAY-jer LEEG) Top-level professional baseball teams.

minor league (MY-ner LEEG) Lower-level professional baseball teams.

practice (PRAK-tiss) Doing something over and over to get better at it.

product (PRAH-dukt) Something that someone sells.

professional (pro-FESH-un-ul) A person who is paid to do something.

scout (SKOWT) A person who looks for good athletes and tells the team that he works for about them.

Index